GROWING PAINS

GRACIE MOSKO

GROWING PAINS

IngramSpark

to my friends at
Thiel College's English Department

CONTENTS

CONTENTS

| 1 |

Growing Pains

"Life will throw sticks and stones at you, it is important to keep on fighting for what you want. Life is going to be rough, and no one has it easy. You will be knocked down numerous times, but you can aways get back up"

PERSEVERE

---

even though
 I am scared
 I am sad
 I am in pain

even though
 I am hurt
 I am lost
 I am confused
still I
 smile wide
 keep on fighting
 grow up trying
still I
 persevere

You deceived me.
I thought you were on my side,
but you deceived me.

You deceived me.
I though you would help me fly,
but you deceived me.

DECEPTION

What if I tried to be like you?

That is,
damaging to my roots,
corrupting my nerves so I can't feel a thing,
paralyzing everything except for my feelings.

You'd like that wouldn't you?

Not just a best friend but a partner in crime,
someone to mess with all of the time,
someone to tell you everything will be fine,
someone to hear all your deceits and your lies,
someone who knows you but needs to say bye.

I can't believe that happened yesterday.
That was humiliating, but hey,
at least I learned something from it.
You can't grow until you fall.

EMBARRASSMENT

Today I tripped walking down the stairs.
The neighbors watched as I tumbled
Down down to the ground.
And no one ran to my rescue,
They just stared.
But it was still a good day

Yesterday I said good morning to someone
At 8 o'clock in the evening,
When the moon replaced the sun.
I walked away humiliated
With tears streaming down my face.
But it was still a good day.

Tomorrow I hope to accomplish
Bigger things than the rest of the days,
But I don't think that will even happen.
Because humans can't grow without trials,
And diamonds aren't made without pain.

PANIC?
NO.
PANIC?
YES?
PANIC.
OH NO!

PANIC

Don't panic.
A tornado is coming.
I hear the pitter-patter noise of rain.
The wind is howling like a pack of wolves.
I have no freedom from this dire mess.
Don't panic.

Don't panic.
A violent tornado came.
I hear that eerie noise around me.
My body is shaking as if an earthquake hit.
My eyes are flooding as if a dam broke free.
My heart is pounding as if a robber broke into
my home.
My brain is broken.

I panicked.

Growing up can be hard, especially when you
encounter change for the first time. Emotions rise up
in you, both fear and excitement. However, once you
embrace that change you are able fly to new heights
and experience a new world.

LITTLE BIRD

___

*fly out of that window
little bird your wings are
trembling in fear*

*where did the time go?
mama bird your baby
can not fly in her tears*

*scared, cold, stuck below.
sweet bird can you hear that
that sweet melody in your ears*

*fly out of that window
little bird your wings are
no longer saturated with fears*

anxiety comes, depression comes, addiction comes
anxiety goes, depression goes, addiction goes

3+2

3+2 equals 5 stress-filled days
Stress-filled days equal stressed out humans
Stressed out humans and anxiety, depression
Anxiety,depression and a blue pill box
A pill box that talks and gets you addicted
Addiction that loves you but makes you
frustrated

1+1 equals 2 stay in bed days
Stay in bed days where the light turns off
The light turns off so you can sleep all day
You get to sleep all day until the days starts
again
3+2 equals 5 stress-filled days

sometimes relationships and friendships are not
what they seem
sometimes relationships and friendships need to
end to make you grow

A DOOR OPENS

A door opens, I follow in with you
We needed each other. You got me and I got
you.
Bad decision, and a bad decision there
And I thought you cared, but there was a wall
up somewhere
Foundations crumble and so do I
Somehow we stopped seeing eye to eye
The walls all broke and so did you
There felt like nothing to hold onto
Moving on with worrying and regret in my
heart
I needed to find a brand new start
Because growing up as a difficult expedition
however, sometimes you need to find a new
mission

it is easy to be oblivious of the blessings that are in front of you.
be open-minded to the good and allow yourself to feel happy

BLIND

I'll take my frustration out on you
You've done nothing wrong I swear

I just don't know what else to do.

I know you help me through thick and thin
I guess I don't see how blessed I am

I think that's why I'm always struggling

Bundles of feelings are flooding my brain
It's permanence is like a big laundry stain

losing someone can be hard
your world is gone in a blink of an eye

COME HOME

____

hurry and come home
i stay up countless nights
staring at the big-box fan
repairing old-dirty kites
hurry and come home

hurry and come home
the scissors sharpened
and clamped my heart
all my happiness has dimmed
hurry and come home

---

listen to your heart, not your head
your head will try to fail you
your heart will lead to love you

RINSE AND REPEAT

---

rewind rinse and repeat
what i thought was best
drowned me in the ocean

rewind rinse and repeat
advice taken and altered
the truth is not the emotion

———————————————

have courage to try new things
have courage to make friends
have courage to accept change

PHONE NUMBER

---

your number is burned into my brain.
10 digits of agony, 10 numbers pain.
do i grab the phone or do I leave it alone?

i am afraid of the life that will follow.
i am afraid of the heartbreak.
i am afraid nothing will change.

there is something that I can not shake
i leave it alone, my thoughts scattered about
will i find pure friendship or am i too late?

embrace your journey
accept change
be unafraid

AUTUMN

---

i saw them tumbling through the grass
what a marvelous thing indeed
red, orange, green, purple and brass
moving at a slow, peaceful speed

these wonderful things do not get a say
on who should stay and who should leave
they gather up to admire and enjoy
then they scatter around in the breeze

———————————————

cherish the little things in life
cherish happy children and today
cherish play and tomorrow

SNOWY DAY

white snowflakes falling beautifully
happy snowmen, part of a community
children laughing in the yard
building igloos standing guard

fingers, toes freezing cold
mom calls out to put play on hold
hot chocolate drinks to warm the spirits
of children, tomorrow will test the limits

---

i promise i will be there for you
whenever you need me to be.

PROMISE

I promise I'm here
When you have a bad day
I promise I'll listen
When you have something to say

I promise I won't leave
when life seems to get hard
I promise I'll cry with you
When love catches you off guard

I promise I'm here
When your plans go awry
I promise I'll listen
Even when you seem shy

_Life is a struggle and we all have hopes and
dreams
sometimes those hopes and dreams take a
different path
and sometimes we do get our dream but it is
such a hard process._

DREAM

---

ran as fast as i can
i saw the finish line
it was a struggle
it was a battle
i crossed that finish line
i did it, i did it
i won

---wait---

i just woke up
i did see the finish line
it was still a struggle
it was still a battle
it was all a dream

____

*Cut out the toxicity in your life.
Get rid of the negatives.
Then you will be truly happy.*

THOUGHTS

As I sit here reflecting I will try to be protecting
My inner peace and love towards myself
What do I do with those thoughts that I keep
having?
The positive thoughts I will keep and shove the
negative ones in a jar
I will toss that jar in the ocean and watch it
float away.
I hear the commotion "Do not leave us, we love
you, we are here for you, no one else
understands"
I wave farewell and the tears runs down my
face,
I realize that what they said to me was not the
case
They were not there for me, they did not love
me, they did not understand.
They were there to distract me, to torment me.
That is why i threw them in the sea

ACKNOWLEDGMENTS

I want to dedicate my first small collection of poetry to the staff of the English Department at Thiel College. I would have never started this collection, let alone finished it, without their support.

Dr. Sheila Gross, thank you for being with me during my most troubling times, guiding me through my struggles, and encouraging me not to give up. I have learned a lot from you, and I plan to carry that with me for a long time.

Prof. Sean Oros, thank you for understanding the traumas that I have gone through and helping me get through them. I have come a long way, and part of it is thanks to you.